Cliff-Hanger

C.J. Vodden

First published in 2006
by C.J. Voden

Cover by Ann Nicholls

ISBN-10: 0-9553873-0-2
ISBN-13: 978-0-9553873-0-2

Printed and bound in Great Britain by
Short Run Press Ltd, Exeter, Devon

CONTENTS

THE DOLPHIN WANTS TO KNOW

Show me your colours
alien from heaven or hell:
what sort of person are you?

Do you love or do you hate,
beg, borrow or steal, and
which way are you?

Show me your colours.

I saw you crying in the slums
and bragging at the palace gates:
what sort of person are you?

Does it matter who you kill or eat,
or if you're honest, if you cheat?
You have the whole world at your feet.

What sort of person are you?
Show me your colours.

THE GIRL WHO SANG THE BLUES ON THE BUS

It was Monday morning on a crowded bus.
You walked upstairs like any normal person.
The bus pulled away
and people stared out of the windows
in a depressed Monday morning way.

You started to sing, softly,
pulling the Blues out of your heart;
singing to yourself at first,
but very soon the whole bus could hear you,
singing the Blues like there was no tomorrow,
spreading your guts all over the floor.

Did someone love you once, somebody care?
Today you're alone, there's nobody there.
I'll never see you again,
the girl who sang the Blues on the bus;
the artist from nowhere, who made life come alive.

CAN DO

Can say
you only changed your mind
and left instead of stayed.

Can watch
while summer turns to rust,
and leaves the spring betrayed.

Can feel
your love behind the door
with every plan we made.

Can clutch
the past, when only time is left,
the game is played.

A QUIET WORD WITH THE MISSILES

I asked the Russian ICBM's
why they were looking so smug,
and they said something in Russian
and then laughed.

I went to the Chinese ICBM's
and asked them why they were looking so smug,
but they answered in Chinese,
and burst out laughing.

So I went over to the British ICBM's and said:
"We speak the same language,
tell me why do you look so smug?"
They gave me a long, hard look and replied:

"You have to be lucky all the time,
we only have to be lucky once;"
and I heard all the missiles throughout the world
laughing and laughing and laughing at their joke.

BURGER

Mince in a bun.
A moment to make,
a moment to eat.
The dejeuner of a man in a hurry.
Food as an inconvenient necessity
to fill the rumbling belly.
No time spent in detailed preparation,
no mysterious tradition
handed down through the mists of time.
Instant, popular, superficial.
The American Dream in one word:
burger.

DAVID

(prognosis: low I.Q., ? schizophrenic)

Young David
small and chubby,
only twenty,
pale and far away as the Arctic,
smiles with broken teeth
black and white,
laughs with or without the joke,
dragging his thoughts along.

He stands hesitantly,
watching,
awkward as a child asking for sweets –
"Can I have a cigarette please?"
Straight to his chair –
flops back – legs cross – uncross,
staring vacantly back.

Talks of Elvis,
and the 'Mr Universe'
he keeps in his locker
along with his dreams.
Day and night
lost in space
with only a cigarette,
staring at heaven.

Sometimes he sings:
broken and plaintive,
like a bird in a cage.

DOCTOR SPECIAL BREW

Good morning, my name's doctor Special Brew,
what can I do for you?

Feeling low, run down, depressed or anxious?
I've got just the tonic to pick you up:

Take a can first thing in the morning,
and last thing at night, and all the hours in between,
and your troubles will disappear (for a while).

You may find yourself living on a park bench,
or in a prison, or in a cemetery,

but that's just unfortunate:
every drug has its side effects.

DISTURBANCE AT THE MAGISTRATE'S COURT

The Magistrates' Court is quiet, sophisticated,
　polite conversation, logical thought;

but from inside the bowels of the building
　come the howls of the damned in hell,

banging on the cells and screaming,
　turning obscenities into madness.

And here we carry on our business,
　orderly, The Law is given and received;

and beneath it all, the voices of the damned,
　the nowhere people with nowhere to go.

MAFIA

You always know where you stand
with the Mafia,
they're so brutally honest.

They tell you to your face
they're going to break your legs
then torture and kill you.

There's no crap about caring,
and how they hate to do it;
you just got unlucky.

The spider waits patiently,
sipping a lager.
Come closer my chosen fly,

and Death glides in silently,
like a dark cloud, with no feelings.

TORTURERS

This is the piece or wire
that gently caresses your innocent body.
Keep still and say your prayers.

This is the electric current
That fills you with energy,
and gives the rest of us a thrill.

Oh! the agony of it, the ecstasy!
Writhing round, contorted body
and the screams – they're so inhuman.

Why do we do it, you ask?
Why not? Because, like Everest
you're there to be climbed.

We have our orders.
Raping you is legal now
inside this heart of darkness.

We have tasted the fruits of hell
and they're delicious:
warm, sweaty, erotic, mad.

Yes, we have become mad dogs
(though we are still our mothers' sons).
Comrades! don't you recognize us?

Look inside the mirror,
look into our faces.
Then shake hands, and pull the switch.

GIRL WITH A PINK CARNATION

Sing me a love song
girl with a pink carnation;

you wear it on your scruffy rucksack,
an invitation to lovers of beauty.

Girl with a pink carnation
where are you going, who are you looking for?

Share a beautiful flower with me,
and I'll carry your rucksack.

PLAY FAIR

Don't drop bombs on naked bums
it's against the Geneva Convention.
If you can shoot a thousand dead,
then raise your arms and say: "I've said – I surrender,"

and not be shot, it's only fair
that some poor snot
crouching in terror on the loo
should say: "Me too – I surrender".

Don't drop your bombs on naked bums,
squatting upon the loo;
it isn't fair, why don't you care?
It's against the Geneva Convention.

(Because, dummy, we'll do whatever it takes to win).

LETTER TO VAN GOGH

Dear Vincent,
I thought I might drop you a line
(since you are now dead
and cannot read the Papers yourself).

They've just sold one of your pictures
for about six million quid.
It was one you did at the end, in the nut-house.
Who would have thought a crazy man
could be worth so much;
either that or they're going crazy
for not knowing the value of money!
What do you think, Vincent?

They put your brain under the hammer,
and all your love and pain
shot around the saleroom
with the echo of a cash register.
What would you have done with the money?
Set up a co-operative for struggling artists?
Given the money to the starving
and splashed out on a new suit?

You've become an investment now, Vincent,
someone's A.1. status.
We still get the dossers like you, the failures,
and put them on drugs
and give them therapy like painting.
Most people avoid them like the plague.
They take their kids round the art gallery
and say: "That's a Van Gogh,
he wasn't really crazy, he was a genius.
The difference my son? Six million quid".

Dear Vincent,
write back if you have the time,
(but don't let it interfere with the painting).

THE CALVES OF MOLTEN METAL
(Exodus 32: 7-14)

———————

Why should we not worship
these calves of molten metal,
these tellies, computers and mobile phones,
machines that make the world go round
and fill our lives with happiness?

Who is this thing that doesn't like it,
peering down from a mountain and
waving an invisible finger, shouting "Fools!".
Who is he (or she) to say we've got it wrong?
And anyway, what's God ever done for us?

THE FLAVOUR OF THE MONTH

It must be great
to be the flavour of the month

and have everyone waiting
on every word the Star can utter.

To be able to do no wrong
because everything is forgiven

the flavour of the month.

To be able to say "It is so",
like God, and only a fool would disagree.

How hard it must be
at the end of the month,

when someone else is the flavour,
and you're the Emperor with no clothes on.

FOOLING IN LOVE

I must be a fool
to fool in love
with a fool like you.

You're a mess,
you have no future
and your past is murky.

Why do fools fool in love?
Is it some disease, like catching the flu?
"No doctor, it's not the flu, the poor fool's in love".

The way you walk, the way you dress,
the way you smile, the things you say,
these foolish things remind me of love.

Fooling in love is fooling for a dream,
a beautiful rainbow always in the distance.
You are my rainbow, and I am your fool.

DEAR JESSICA

Dear Jessica,
this is a poem just for you.

You don't deserve it
because you've been a bad girl

playing with naughty toys
like drugs.

Dear Jessica,
you always were an actress,

a naughty girl
who played the system

and got your fingers badly burnt
and had the money to buy your way out.

Dear Jessica,
you loved the dreamy painters,

and your corruption
was always tainted with innocence.

My child, how can God refuse you,
Jessica,

crying in the sweetness of your hell
for God to take you away:

and He will, 'cause life is not like that.

WHY DO LEMMINGS

Why do lemmings commit suicide?
Do they suddenly realize
there is no God
and life is pointless,
or do they just go along with the crowd?
Is there some leader who starts it all
and says: "Sod this for a game of lemmings
we're going over the top",
who puts it all down to instinct
or population control,
the deaths of millions of lemmings?

There were millions of lemmings in 1914
who followed the crowd
and were marching gaily to their deaths.
Were their leaders wise
or were the lemmings misinformed?
After all, it was the fashionable thing to do,
and only brave men and fools
refuse to conform.

THE HOOKER

Never let it be said
that I was only using you,
I needed a piece of meat
to lay my eggs in.

You were what I needed
to aid my insecurity,
and like the mosquito
I sucked your blood while you were sleeping.

You're getting a little itchy?
Tough luck!
Now you know how it is
when you're lifted by a hooker:

I get the blood, and you get the itch.

PARANOIA

It's no use trying to get me,
I'm watching you.

You have my letters, I know,
but there's nothing in them.

I saw you watching me
when I crossed the road,

I heard the echoes of your conversation
in the other room,

and I know that there's a plot.
You've got nothing on me

so you may as well give up.
I'm watching you watching me.

I WENT TO SEE THE PRIEST

I went to see the priest
and he said:

"I can walk down the Fulham Road
and most people I meet
don't know who they are
or where they've come from
or where they're going;
and what's more,
if I asked them
they wouldn't understand the question".

He said:
"We all have two basic needs,
to be loved
and to be forgiven.
Bless you my son,
go in peace".

LOVE YOU

How much do I love you?
More than I can ever tell you.

More than all the tea in China,
More than all the fishes in the sea.

So don't ask how much I love you;
I love you more than words can ever say.

CHRIST STOPPED AT EBOLI

Christ stopped at Eboli,
and also at 10 Downing Street;
he said: "This is as far as I can come
with my good news, with the light of love;
darkness begins at Eboli."

I saw him crying on the pavement,
and put my arm around him.
He turned into a homeless person.
I said: "Jesus, it's only life,
you have your own kingdom."

He kissed me softly on the cheek,
and so far, I have not betrayed him.

TIGHTENING THE SCREWS

Tightening the screws is a subtle game
played by those with the best education,
and a sense of evil to provide motivation:
money, power, status, what more could a man want?
Turn the screws; it's not your pain, or your children's.

Poor people have become a disease,
a cancer in the body politic
to be rooted out and found a place
near the dustbin. You will find many people there,
clinging to their broken dreams and their children,

wondering why it had to happen to them.

And why should it not happen to them, I ask you,
if life is a struggle for survival,
a struggle to get on?
Who cares for the helpless and the pathetic,
and why?

It's all tied up in the game that we belong to,
and the shadow of hell is a long piece of darkness.
Some people still have love, but it's a dying art
in a world that measures a man by his credit card.
Evil is so ordinary it becomes a way of life,

until the final screams are heard only by God.

WHAT DID THE PREACHER SAY?

It was all the same to you,
you said, and you didn't give a shit.
"They can all stuff it", you said,
"and may they rot in hell".

"No one tells me what to do"
you said, gazing into the mirror.
"I'll bloody well show them they
can't walk all over me!"

I looked out of the window
and saw the falling leaves of autumn.
Vanity of vanities,
and all is vanity.

SAY YOU LOVE ME

Say – do you love me?
Say it again.

I never knew
until you told me to my face –

do you love me?

I was so unloveable
until you said the magic words –

say you love me,
say it again.

Say it until I have to believe you,
me, alone, with only you to give me hope.

THE KILLING FLOOR

Where do you live, my son?
I live on the killing floor.

What do you believe, my son?
I believe in survival.

Where are you going, my son?
I am going to my grave.

Where is love, my son?
It lies inside a broken heart.

Are you cynical, my son?
I have seen heaven turn into hell.

Why do you weep, my son?

Why do you not answer me?

BROKEN DOWN FRIENDS

Friends are great to have,
but they shouldn't keep breaking down
like an old Ford Popular.

I thought they were built to last,
but they throw a wobbly one
and break with the strain of living.

Friends, who'd have them,
what can you do with them,
breaking up all over the place?

Like china dolls they're fragile,
like puppies they need affection,
like the Mona Lisa they need armour plating.

Friends, you can't get rid of them,
they're like some disease that does you good;
you bring them flowers

and they cry all over your handkerchief
with a sad sob story
that you once told a year ago.

It's sad to have friends cracking up,
but you have them or you don't;
and if you do, hold them close,
and gather their tears like holy water.

MISSING YOU

The days are passing slowly.
You went away a long time ago.
I miss you, kiss you in my dreams –
it's been so long

so long for lovers.
Try to see my eyes that hide the cry –
"I'm missing you!" – It must be said –
so long ago you said goodbye,

goodbye.
How you make me cry.
And time and time again
I search the mirror, wonder – why?

C'EST LA VIE

"C'est la vie
c'est la guerre
c'est la mort –"

"Say no more,
say no more."

DETOX

There are no John Waynes in a detox.,
only chickens.

When your body screams at you
you scream back.
Welcome to the club, my friend,
hell is where you live,
for a while it's going to be home.

Pain is very personal,
like a lover it knows all your tender spots.

Welcome to the wonderful world of detox.
May you die happier than you're living.

PRACTISING THE PERFECT GOODBYE

Goodbye was all he had to say,
the sad man, who died today:
goodbye.
he had nothing more to say.

He said a sad farewell
to the children eating ice-creams,
and then it was the corpse
that said goodbye, and died without a whisper.

AN ATHEIST FAREWELL

We are both old
the lady said,
and my husband's been to hospital,
I can see it in his eyes
that he's going to leave me soon.

I wouldn't mind
if I believed
that we would be together later,
but I think that when we part
I shall not see him again.

And it now seems
that life is cruel
to leave me once again all alone;
I'm just glad that I have shared
Something wonderful with him.

THE KILLING FIELDS

Billions of bones
like dead branches
are scattered throughout
the killing fields of history.

Every bone was once
a mother's child
or a lover's limb
that once caressed.

Mothers are left
to see their children
Lying trampled on the ground
like broken flowers,

and shed billions of tears
on their graves, like rain,
to bring back the blossoms
that once were so precious.

Nothing grows in the killing fields
except death.
The bones lie cold and feel nothing,
like coal.

EASTER FRIDAY

Easter Friday is the dock-end of life,
the grotty filter full of cancer.
The time of sadness and pain,
of sympathy and love.

Has someone died, is it important?
No one told me, how was I to know
in a world of Easter eggs
and late night parties?

Is it over or has it just begun,
this awful death?
has anyone told his mother?
Who is this who screams for pain to go away

and cries
"Never do this to me again"?

COMING HOME

It's cold out here
and I want to come home.

Give us a break, will yer,
I want to come home.

I've been frozen for many years
and the snow just keeps getting colder,

I want to come home.

Love has disappeared into the night
and left me with darkness and pain,

and the good days are when the snow
starts to melt and cover me with rain.

It's time I came home.

OLD MAN

("... and you will end up in one room, alone, with nothing".)

When I was young
when I was young,
Oh I was full of fun
when I was young.

When I was young
I used to ride the world
and climb up to the stars,
living between the woods and Mars.

But now I grow old,
and what has become of my years?
There is pain in my eyes
as memories dissolve into tears.

Soon I shall walk in the park;
while children feed the pigeons.

DON'T HANG JESUS

Don't hang Jesus,
put him in a zoo.

The Americans will pay to see him
and say: "Gee, I didn't know he was so small,

doesn't he smell, is he on the dole?
How pathetic – don't go too near, children."

Poor Jesus, he got the timing wrong
and ended up in a zoo.

Still, at least the children will get to see him,
feeding him nuts –

"Mummy, why is that man always crying?"

KNOW THAT I AM PERFECT

———————

I am the beauty in a flower,
the anger in a thunderstorm;
I am perfect
because I am God,
and if I were not perfect
I would not be God.

You see me very vaguely, Cliff,
you don't try hard enough.
Look at me,
and **know** that I am perfect.